Put Beginning Readers on the Right Track with
ALL ABOARD READING™

The All Aboard Reading series is especially designed for beginning readers. Written by noted authors and illustrated in full color, these are books that children really want to read—books to excite their imagination, expand their interests, make them laugh, and support their feelings. With fiction and nonfiction stories that are high interest and curriculum-related, All Aboard Reading books offer something for every young reader. And with four different reading levels, the All Aboard Reading series lets you choose which books are most appropriate for your children and their growing abilities.

Picture Readers
Picture Readers have super-simple texts, with many nouns appearing as rebus pictures. At the end of each book are 24 flash cards—on one side is a rebus picture; on the other side is the written-out word.

Station Stop 1
Station Stop 1 books are best for children who have just begun to read. Simple words and big type make these early reading experiences more comfortable. Picture clues help children to figure out the words on the page. Lots of repetition throughout the text helps children to predict the next word or phrase—an essential step in developing word recognition.

Station Stop 2
Station Stop 2 books are written specifically for children who are reading with help. Short sentences make it easier for early readers to understand what they are reading. Simple plots and simple dialogue help children with reading comprehension.

Station Stop 3
Station Stop 3 books are perfect for children who are reading alone. With longer text and harder words, these books appeal to children who have mastered basic reading skills. More complex stories captivate children who are ready for more challenging books.

In addition to All Aboard Reading books, look for All Aboard Math Readers™ (fiction stories that teach math concepts children are learning in school) and All Aboard Science Readers™ (nonfiction books that explore the most fascinating science topics in age-appropriate language).

All Aboard for happy reading!

AN ALL ABOARD READING™ COLLECTION

Station Stop 3

EXTREME NATURE

Grosset & Dunlap

**The All Aboard Station Stop 3 Collection:
EXTREME NATURE published in 2003.**

Published by Grosset & Dunlap, a division of Penguin Young Readers Group, 345 Hudson Street, New York, NY, 10014.
ALL ABOARD READING and GROSSET & DUNLAP are trademarks of Penguin Group (USA) Inc. Published simultaneously in Canada. Printed in the U.S.A.

ISBN 0-448-43337-0   A B C D E F G H I J

Extreme Nature

By Dana del Prado, Jennifer Dussling,
Gail Herman, and Nicholas Nirgiotis

Illustrated by Stephen Marchesi, Denise Ortakales,
Lori Osiecki, Michael Radencich, and Larry Schwinger

Grosset & Dunlap
New York

TABLE OF CONTENTS

LIGHTNING

It's Electrifying

By Jennifer Dussling
Illustrated by Lori Osiecki

On November 9, 1965, a full moon
rose into the dark sky over New York
City. It was just after five o'clock. The
city sparkled with lights in offices and
apartments, restaurants and stores.
Red and green streetlights blinked
on and off as thousands of cars, buses,
and taxis hurried through the city.

All of a sudden, everything changed.

Miles north of New York City,
something went wrong in the giant
conductor lines that brought power to the
city. In minutes, New York City lost all its
electricity. The lights went out. Elevators
were stuck between floors. Subway trains
stopped dead in their tracks.

There was a total blackout!

The entire city was shut down for over ten hours. Six hundred thousand people were trapped in the subway. In the Empire State Building alone, thirteen elevators remained jam-packed with people. The city's traffic lights weren't working. Cars didn't know when to stop or go.

And all because something went wrong with the electric power.

Until it is gone, most people don't realize how important electricity is. Think about your own house. How many things plug in? Lamps. TV. Microwave oven. Toaster. Stereos. VCR. Computer. Without electricity, none of them will work.

Electricity is the energy that runs many things in our everyday lives. It is hard to explain exactly what electricity is. And for something so important, electricity starts in a small way.

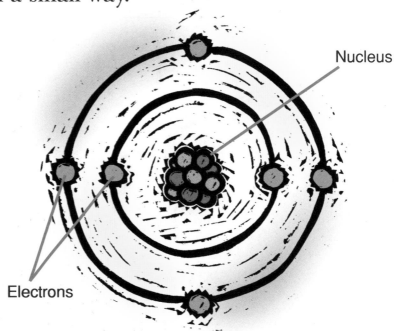

Nucleus

Electrons

Everything in the world is made of tiny bits called atoms. Houses. Trees. Food. Air. Water. Books. Animals. Even you! You are made of atoms. Electricity happens because of atoms.

Atoms are too tiny to be seen. Yet atoms are made up of even smaller particles. The particles have electrical charges. One kind of particle is called a nucleus. (You say it like this—NOO-klee-uss.) It is in the center of the atom. It has a positive charge. Other particles in the atom are called electrons. (You say it like this—ee-LECK-tronz.) Electrons have negative charges. The positive charge of the nucleus pulls at the negative charges in the electrons.

In some atoms, the pull is very strong. The electrons are held very tightly. Yet, in other atoms, the pull is weak. Sometimes the electrons can escape from the atom and travel to other atoms. This happens in certain metals like copper. A stream of electrons travelling through atoms of copper or other metals is what makes electricity.

Large power plants create electricity. Metal coils within giant magnets are turned by water or steam. This makes electrons run through wire and move from one atom to another.

The wires take this electricity from the power plant to towns and cities across the country. Some of these cables go right into your house. Just think—you are linked up to a huge power plant!

The wires that bring electricity to you
are actually made of two smaller wires.
One wire takes electricity into your
house. The other takes it out of your
house and back to the power plant. The
cable is like a two-way loop between your
house and the power plant.

If the loop is broken, electricity will not flow. That is what happened on a big, big scale in New York City during the 1965 blackout. This is also what happens every time you turn off a light switch in your house. That's because smaller loops connect the light switches in your house to the large loop. When you turn off a switch, it breaks the loop. Flip the switch on. The loop is complete again. The electricity can flow once more.

Most of the time, you do not see
electricity. You only see what it can do.
But there is one time when you can't miss
it. That's because one type of electricity
isn't made by power plants. It happens
in nature. Can you guess what it is?

Lightning.

Lightning is a big, hot stream of electricity. One bolt of lightning is brighter than a billion light bulbs. It is white-hot. It travels at speeds of up to 60,000 miles per hour and one bolt can be from six to ten miles long. Yet it is only about as wide as your finger.

Lightning can start a fire on the ground. It can burn down a house. It can split a tree. If it hits a person, it may kill him. Each year, about 350 people get hit by lightning in the United States. That may seem like a lot. But there are about 287 million people in the country! It is very unlikely you will ever be struck by lightning.

Lightning can play some funny tricks. It can blow the clothes right off a person's back. Once it hit a man inside a sleeping bag and melted the zipper shut. Scientists don't know why lightning does such weird things. But they do know a little about what makes lightning happen.

23

Lightning begins in a big storm cloud. The cloud can be six miles high! Ice crystals and raindrops inside the cloud quickly move back and forth and up and down. All this movement makes an electrical charge in the cloud. The charge wants to escape from the cloud.

Meanwhile, in the ground under the cloud, another charge builds up. Scientists don't know quite why this happens. But they do know that the charge in the cloud and the charge in the ground want to meet. Sparks begin to shoot down from the cloud and up from the ground in streams. When the stream from the cloud meets the stream from the ground, it makes a lightning bolt.

This may be hard to understand. But did you ever rub a balloon against your hair? Do you remember what happens? When you take the balloon away, your hair stretches out toward the balloon. Both your hair and the balloon have an electrical charge. They want to meet up. The same thing happens between the cloud and the ground. And lightning bridges the gap.

The balloon and your hair have a kind of natural electricity. You have probably felt it another way, too. Sometimes if you walk across a carpet and touch a metal doorknob, you get a little shock. You may even see sparks. This kind of electricity is called static electricity.

Lightning is like static electricity. It jumps between a cloud and the ground like the sparks jump between your hand and the doorknob. But not all lightning jumps from a cloud to the ground.

Lightning can hop between clouds.
Or lightning can happen within a cloud.
This is called in-cloud lightning. You may
have seen it before. The cloud flickers
with light and seems to glow from inside.

There is maybe one other kind of lightning. You will probably never see it. In fact, some scientists are not sure it even exists. No one knows what causes it. It is called ball lightning. Ball lightning is a bright spark that floats in the air. It is red or yellow and about the size of your head. Most lightning moves very quickly. Ball lightning moves much more slowly. It lasts a second or two and then explodes with a loud POP!

In the 1800s, a man told a story about ball lightning. A fiery ball floated into his house. It came toward him. It rose straight up, then it darted into a stovepipe and traveled through the chimney. At the top of the chimney, it exploded, knocking off chunks of stone and brick.

So how did anyone ever figure out
that lightning is electricity? For a long
time nobody made the connection. For
thousands of years, people believed
lightning came from angry gods.

The Viking people believed in Thor,
the god of thunder. He had an angry
temper. Lightning sparked when Thor
struck his hammer against his anvil.

The Aztec people
of Mexico thought
that a god named
Tlaloc threw
lightning bolts.

In ancient Egypt,
Seth was the god
of storms and
lightning.

The ancient Chinese had a god named Lei Kung. He had wings, a bird head, and blue skin. He made thunder with his hammers.

In ancient Greece,
people believed that Zeus
was the king of all the gods.
He threw lightning bolts
at evil people from his
palace in the sky.

It took a long, long time for anyone to connect electricity with lightning. It was not until 1752 that someone proved that lightning was electricity. That someone was Ben Franklin.

Over hundreds of years, scientists had figured out some things about electricity. They knew electricity passed easily through metal. They also knew it didn't pass through things like silk and wax. Ben Franklin took this information and made up an experiment.

Ben was worried his experiment might not work. Ben was afraid other scientists might make fun of him. So he told his plan only to his 21-year-old son.

Ben found a large silk handkerchief and two sticks. He put them together to make a kite. Ben tied a pointed metal rod to the kite. He ran a long cord up to the kite. At the other end, Ben put a metal key. Then he tied a silk string to the end of the cord. Ben held on to the silk string. He knew the silk would keep the lightning from hurting him.

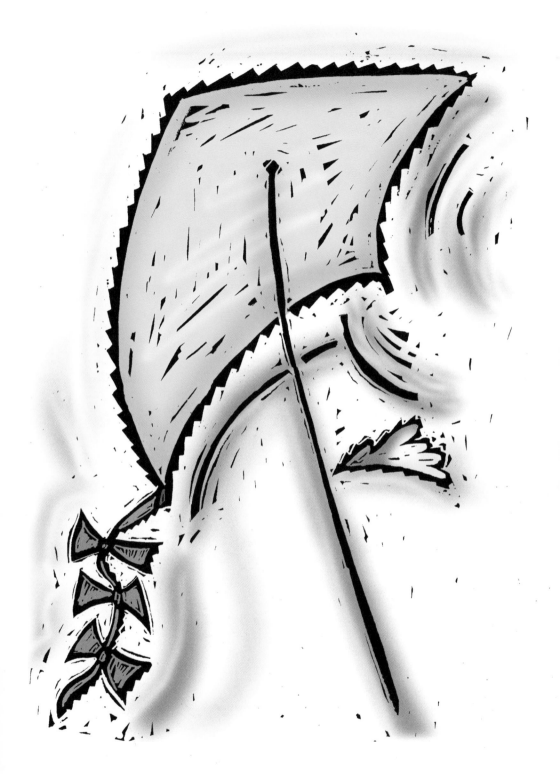

On a June day in 1752, Ben and his son saw a summer thunderstorm come up. They stood under a shed. The shed kept them—and the silk string—dry. From there Ben flew the kite. They waited for lightning to strike the kite.

When it did, it traveled down the cord. Just as electricity passes into

metal, the lightning passed into the
metal key. When Ben put his finger
near the key, a spark jumped to it.
(Don't try this!) Ben was a smart man,
but he did some very dangerous things!
However, with this experiment,
Ben Franklin proved that lightning
is electricity.

Because of his discovery, Ben was able
to make an invention that prevented many
fires. Most houses were made of wood. If
they got hit by lightning, the houses
caught on fire and burned down.

Ben knew lightning seeks a way to the
ground. It also usually strikes the highest
thing around. And he knew it passes easily
through metal. So in 1753, Ben Franklin
made the first lightning rod.

He attached a metal rod to a house. Then he ran metal wires from the rod down along the side of the house and into the ground. The lightning rod worked perfectly. When a thunderstorm was overhead, lightning hit the rod, not the house. The electricity then passed down the wires and into the ground. No one was hurt. The house didn't burn.

This idea explains why it's safe to be inside a metal car (with the windows rolled up) during a thunderstorm. The car is like a lightning rod. The electricity travels through the metal without hurting anyone inside.

But what do you do if you are not in a house or car during a storm?

Stay away from big trees and telephone poles and wire fences. Stay away from hills and open fields. Get out of any water. If you're stuck outside, crouch down. Don't lie down. Don't put your hands on the ground. If you put your hands on the ground, you would make a loop with the ground like the loop of wire that carries electricity to your house. Then the charge might pass through you to the ground and back up through you again!

One other place to avoid during a storm is a wet beach. But check out the beach after the storm is gone. You may find a fulgurite.

A what?

Fulgurites (FULL-geh-rites) are sometimes called "fossil lightning." They are twisted, crusty tubes of glass. Lightning is so hot that when it strikes a beach, it melts the sand into glass. The biggest fulgurite ever found was in South Amboy, New Jersey. It was nine feet long and three inches wide.

Since lightning is very hot, it heats up the air around the bolt. The air expands quickly, then cools again quickly. This quick change makes a sharp crack. Can you guess what that is?

The sound is thunder. Sometimes you hear thunder the moment you see lightning. But sometimes you see a flash of lightning first and hear the thunder a couple of seconds later. That's because light travels faster than sound. So if the storm is near you, you will see the lightning and hear the thunder at the same time. But if the storm is farther away, you don't hear the thunder until a little later.

It takes the sound of thunder five seconds to travel one mile. You can tell how far away the storm is by counting the time between when you see the lightning and when you hear the thunder. Count "one Mississippi, two Mississippi, three Mississippi . . ." until you hear the thunder. (It takes about one second to say "one Mississippi.") So if you get to "five Mississippi," the storm is a mile away.

There are 44,000 thunderstorms every day on Earth. Every day lightning strikes millions of times. And lightning is not on Earth alone. Scientists think there is lightning on other planets, too, like Jupiter and Venus!

Electricity is all around us. Until a few hundred years ago, it was just a mystery. It was something people watched in the sky. It was something to be afraid of, something that could burn down a house. But today we know how amazing electricity is. It makes our lives easier. It makes our lives brighter.

At 4:44 in the morning on November 10, 1965, electricity returned to New York City. The subways started running. The elevators began to work. Street lights blinked red and green and yellow again. Most people were asleep when the power came on. But when they woke up, they were very happy to have it back.

So where would we be
without electricity?
In the dark!

PLANETS

By Jennifer Dussling
Illustrated by Denise Ortakales

Long ago, in Greece,
people looked at the night sky.
They saw the moon.
They saw bright stars.

They also saw other objects
that moved across the sky.
They called them planetes.
In Greek that means wanderer.
That's where we get the word "planet."

We live on the planet called Earth.
Earth circles the sun.
So do eight other planets.

Uranus

Pluto

Jupiter

Neptune

Saturn

The sun and the nine planets
are called the solar system.

For a long time people thought that
the sun circled Earth!
One man said that was wrong.
His name was Copernicus.
(You say it like this—coe-purr-nuh-kuss.)
In 1513, he had a new idea.
He said that Earth circled the sun.

He wrote a book about it.
The book did not come out
until thirty years later!
Most people thought that
his idea was crazy.
But Copernicus was right.
The sun is the center
of the solar system.

Each planet has its own path
around the sun.
The paths are not really circles.
They are more like ovals.
The paths are called orbits.

The time it takes for a planet
to travel around the sun is a year.
An Earth year is 365 days.
Planets also spin.
A day is the time it takes for a planet
to make a complete spin.
On Earth a day is
twenty-four hours long.

Mercury is the closest planet
to the sun.
It circles the sun in eighty-eight days.
So on Mercury,
a year is only eighty-eight days long.
How old are you in Mercury years?
Mercury is a small planet
with craters and cliffs.
It has no moons.
Mercury gets very hot during the day
and very cold at night.

The next planet is Venus.
You can see it
in the morning sky.
It looks white and beautiful.
Long ago,
Romans named
the planets after their gods.
We still use the Roman names.

Mercury was the messenger
of the gods.

Venus was
the goddess of beauty.

Mars was the god
of war.

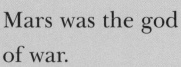

Venus is the hottest planet.
The temperature on Venus is 900° F!
That is much hotter than an oven.
Why is Venus hotter than Mercury?
After all, Mercury is closer to the sun.

It is hotter because
Venus is covered
with thick yellow clouds.
They keep in the heat
like a blanket.

Earth is the third planet from the sun.
Earth is the only planet with life on it—
people, animals, and plants.
It is in the perfect place,
not too close to the sun
and not too far away.
On Earth we have plenty of water.
Without water there can be no life.
Earth also has a thin layer
of gases around it.
This is the air we breathe.
These gases also block out
harmful light from the sun.

The planet after Earth is Mars.
Mars has dusty red soil.
The red dust in the air
makes the sky look pink.
Sometimes Mars has dust storms
that last for months.
Can you guess why the red planet
was named after the war god?
It is because red is the color of blood.

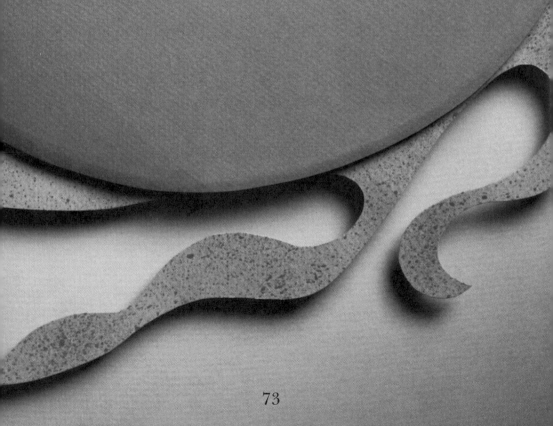

There are a lot of stories about little green men from Mars. They are not true.

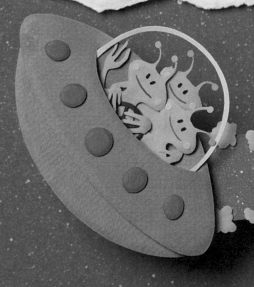

True

Not True

But at one time,
maybe there was some kind of life on Mars.
In 1996, a little rock made big news.
Scientists found the rock in Antarctica.
Long ago it had fallen from Mars.
The rock had a fossil in it,
a fossil of tiny cells.
Because of this,
some scientists think that
there may have been
some kind of life on Mars.

Mars also has ice caps
and channels that
may have carried water.
Why is that so important?
Because all living things need water.

So some scientists think that
maybe people could live on Mars.
Maybe some day far in the future,
we will build a city there!

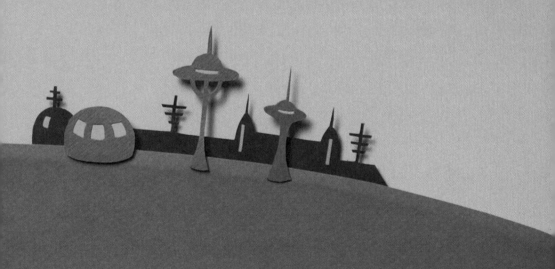

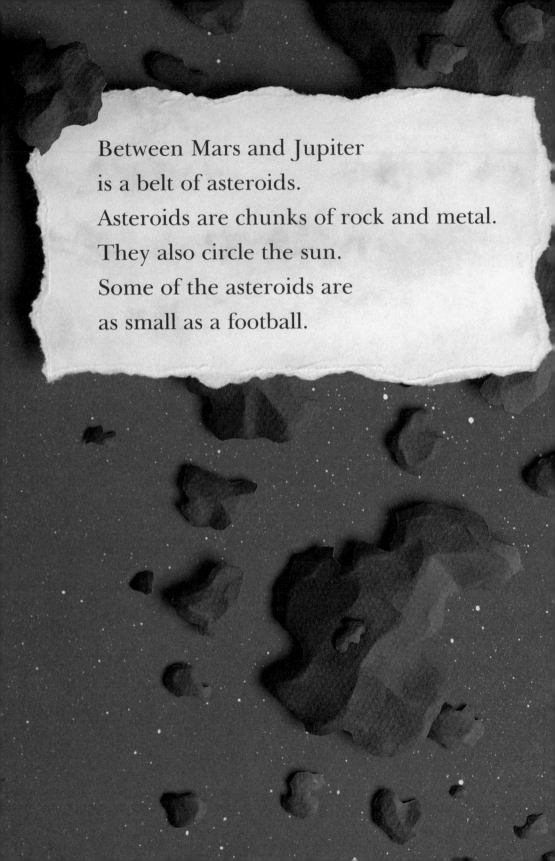

Between Mars and Jupiter
is a belt of asteroids.
Asteroids are chunks of rock and metal.
They also circle the sun.
Some of the asteroids are
as small as a football.

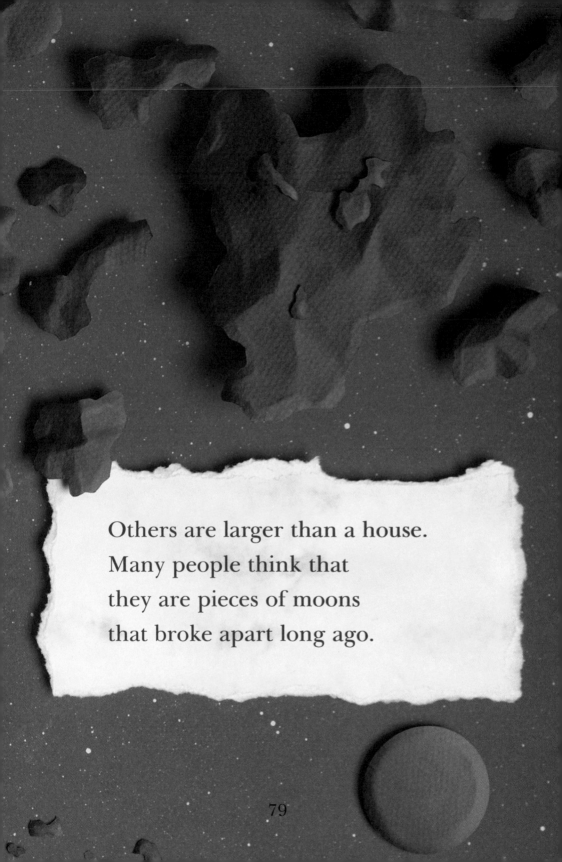

Others are larger than a house.
Many people think that
they are pieces of moons
that broke apart long ago.

Jupiter is the fifth planet from the sun.

Jupiter is huge!

It is the largest planet in the solar system.

It is much larger than Earth.

Think of Jupiter and Earth like this:

If Earth were the size of a pea,

Jupiter would be the size of an orange.

Jupiter doesn't look at all like
Mercury, Venus, Earth, or Mars.
Jupiter is made mostly of gas, not rock.
So are the next three planets—
Saturn, Uranus, and Neptune.

Saturn

Uranus

Neptune

Jupiter

Jupiter is a stormy place.
See the red circle on Jupiter?
That is called the Great Red Spot.
It is like a super hurricane.
Strong winds blow.
Lightning bolts crack
through the clouds.
This storm has been raging
for hundreds of years!

Earth is not the only planet with a moon.
Jupiter has at least sixteen!

How is a moon different from a planet?
A moon orbits a planet.
It does not orbit the sun.

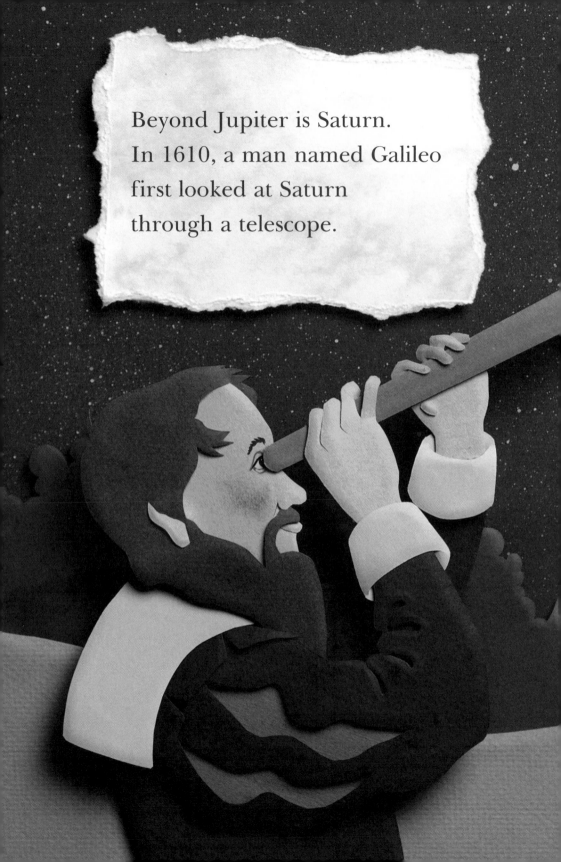

Beyond Jupiter is Saturn.
In 1610, a man named Galileo
first looked at Saturn
through a telescope.

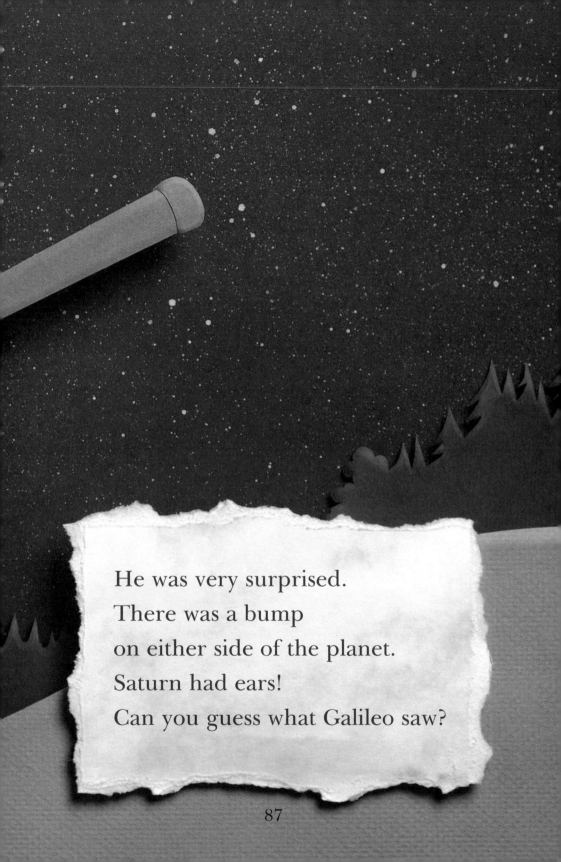

He was very surprised.
There was a bump
on either side of the planet.
Saturn had ears!
Can you guess what Galileo saw?

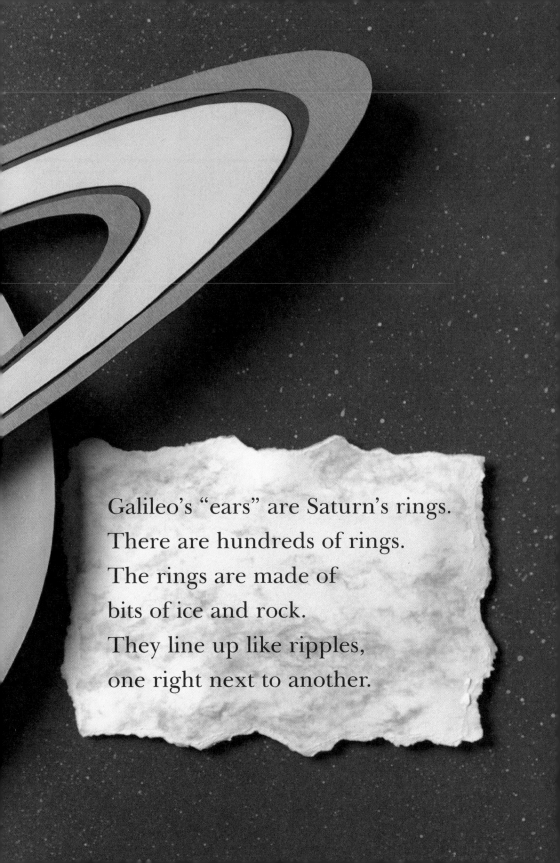

Galileo's "ears" are Saturn's rings.
There are hundreds of rings.
The rings are made of
bits of ice and rock.
They line up like ripples,
one right next to another.

For hundreds of years
people thought that
Saturn was the only planet
with rings around it.
But it's not.
Uranus, the seventh planet,
does too.
Its rings are made
of chunks of black rocks.
Uranus is a tippy planet.
It lies on its side.

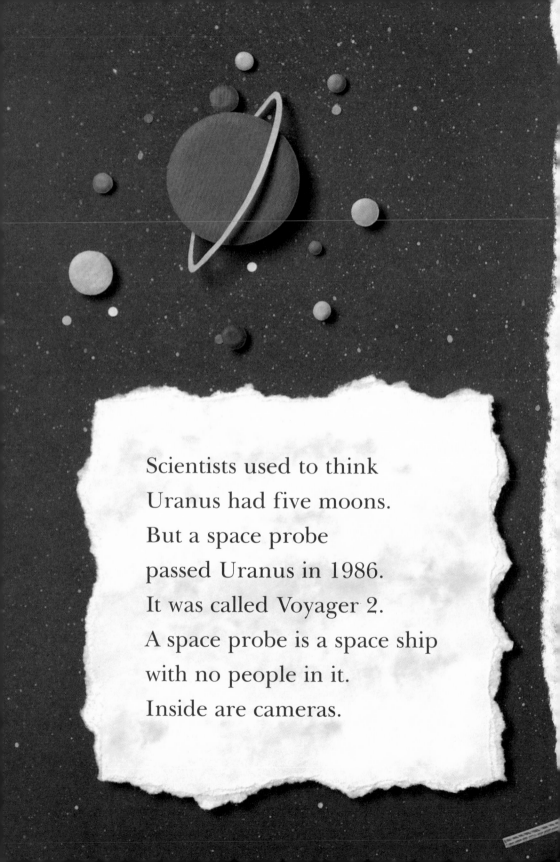

Scientists used to think
Uranus had five moons.
But a space probe
passed Uranus in 1986.
It was called Voyager 2.
A space probe is a space ship
with no people in it.
Inside are cameras.

The cameras on Voyager 2
took lots of pictures
and sent them to Earth.
The pictures showed
many more moons
near Uranus.
They also showed that
Uranus had rings.

Neptune was the god of the sea.
He could whip up storms
on the water.

So Neptune is a good name
for the next planet.
It is blue–green
and it has the fastest winds
on any planet.
They can reach 700 miles an hour.
Neptune sometimes has a spot—
the Great Dark Spot.
It is another huge storm.

The planet Pluto was not
found until 1930.
It is a small planet.
It is very cold.
That is because it is so far
from the sun.
It takes Pluto 248 years
to travel once
around the sun.

Pluto

Neptune

Pluto has a very strange orbit.
For twenty years out of the 248,
Pluto travels inside Neptune's orbit.
During that time,
Neptune becomes the farthest planet
from the sun.

Because it's so small
and has a crazy orbit,
some scientists think that
Pluto was once a moon of Neptune.
But somehow it went into its own orbit.
So, is Pluto really a planet?
Some scientists don't think so.

They want to drop Pluto
from the list of planets.
Then the solar system
will have only eight planets.
But other scientists think that
Pluto is a planet.
For now, Pluto is still listed as a planet.

What is out there past Pluto?

Lots and lots of stars.

Lots of other solar systems.

We've sent probes past Pluto.

They are headed to the faraway stars.

Who knows what they will find!

Volcanoes

Mountains That Blow Their Tops

By Nicholas Nirgiotis
Illustrated by Michael Radencich

It is a quiet day on an island.
Or so it seems.

Suddenly a mountain starts to shake.
Clouds of smoke shoot from the top.
The mountain smokes for days and days.

Then it happens!
KABOOM!
The mountain blows its top!
A red-hot cloud of ash bursts out.
It burns the town in minutes.

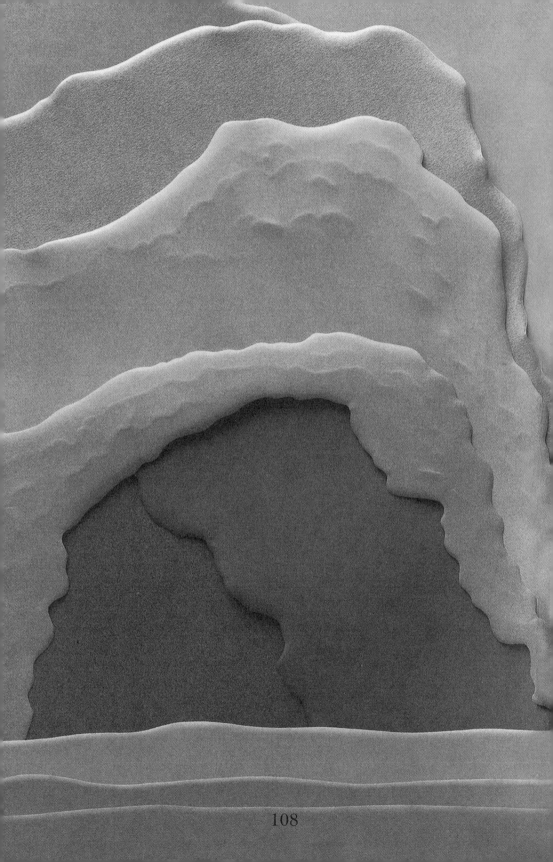

Just two people get away.
One is a girl.
She knows a cave.
She used to play there.
She takes a boat to the cave.
She is safe.

The other is a man.
He is safe in a jail
underground.
This is a true story.
It happened in 1902.
Mont Pelée is the name
of the mountain.
(You say it like this:
mont pe-LAY.)

Florida

It is on the island of
Martinique
in the Atlantic Ocean.
Mont Pelée is a special
kind of mountain—
it is a volcano.

Atlantic Ocean

Martinique

South America

Long ago, people thought
a god of fire lived inside volcanoes.
They thought he liked
to move from one volcano to another.
Every time he moved
he stirred things up.
Today we know the facts.
Volcanoes start deep in the earth.

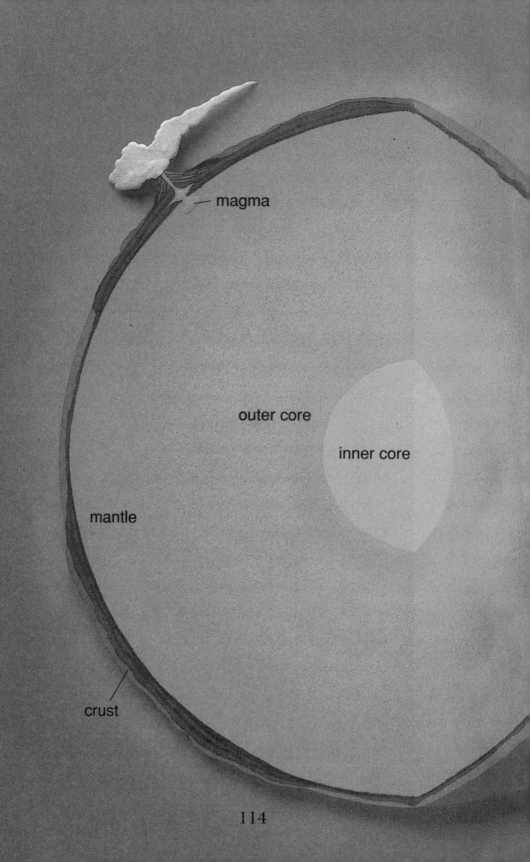

magma

outer core

inner core

mantle

crust

The earth is round—
like an orange.
It is made of layers
of rock.
The top layer is called
the crust.
It is like the skin
of the orange.
The layer below
is called the mantle.
The mantle is very hot.
So some of the rock melts.
The melted rock is
called magma.

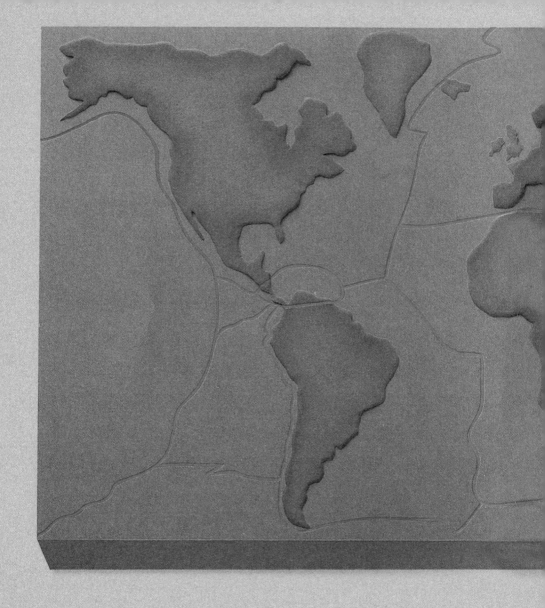

The top layers of earth are made up
of many pieces.
These pieces are called plates.
The red lines show where the plates meet.
This is where most volcanoes happen.

The plates are always moving—
very, very slowly!
Some plates push against each other.
Some plates pull away
from each other.

The magma is moving too.
It pushes up on the plates.
Sometimes the magma
finds a crack
between the plates.

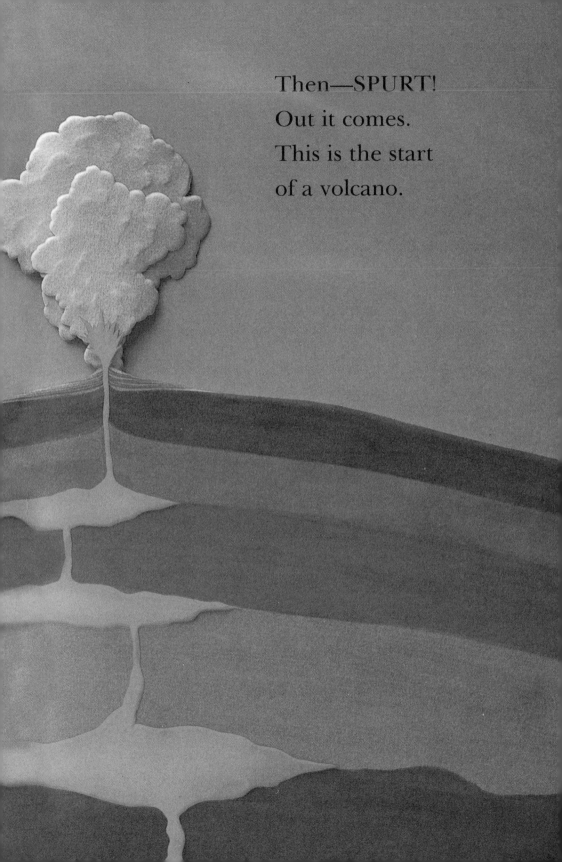

Then—SPURT!
Out it comes.
This is the start
of a volcano.

The magma bubbles up a tube.

The tube is like a long straw.

At the top is a hole.

The hole is called a crater.

The magma spills out of the crater.

Now the magma is called lava.

There are two kinds of lava.
One kind is soft and runny—
and red hot!
It flows in fast, fiery rivers
from the volcano.

As the lava cools,
it turns back into smooth rock.

The other kind of lava
flows much more slowly.
Sometimes it sprays out
of the crater into the sky.
In the air the lava hardens
into sharp rocks and ash.
Then black clouds of ash
fill the sky.
They block out the sun,
so it is dark—
even at noon!

Not many people get to see
a volcano being born.
But fifty years ago,
one boy did.
He lived in Mexico.
One day he was helping
his father on their farm.

Suddenly the earth split open.
Smoke and ash shot into the air.
The boy and his father ran
to warn the people in town.

Ash and rock kept shooting up.
A hill started to grow.

By the next day,
the hill was as tall
as ten houses.

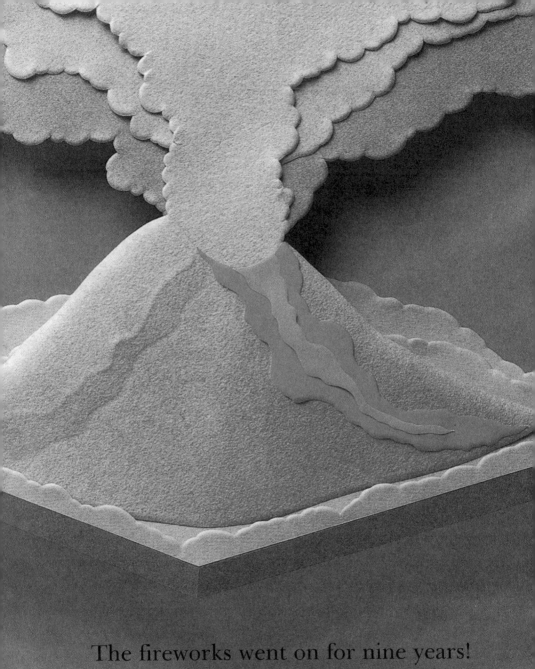

The fireworks went on for nine years!
The farm was gone.
The town was gone.
In their place was a new volcano.

Some volcanoes start
at the bottom of the sea,
where no one can see them.
The ocean floor splits open.
Hot lava pours out.

The lava cools and hardens.
The volcano grows.
Slowly it rises above the water.
This is how some islands are made.

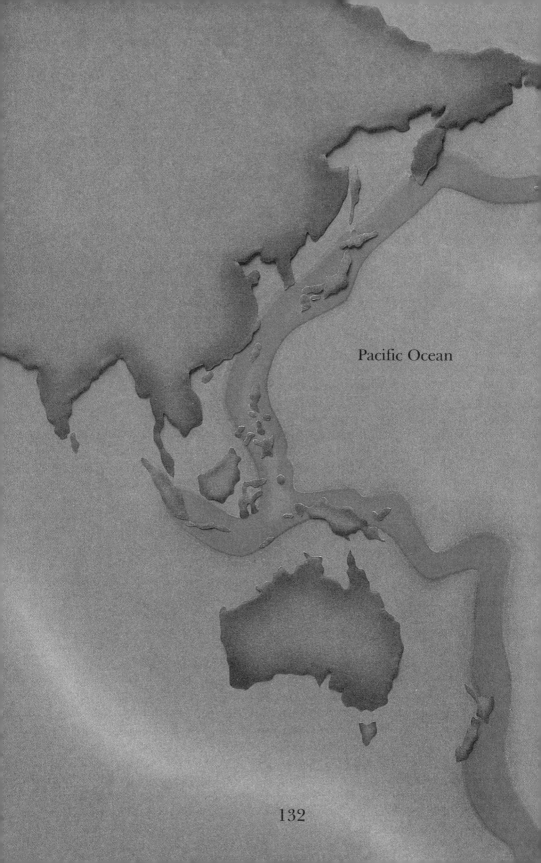

Pacific Ocean

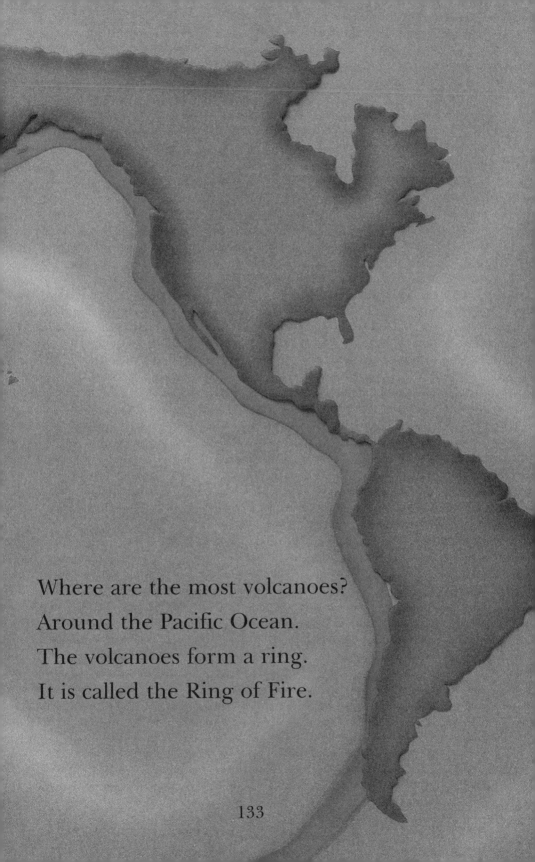

Where are the most volcanoes?
Around the Pacific Ocean.
The volcanoes form a ring.
It is called the Ring of Fire.

Are there volcanoes in the United States?
Yes.
Mount St. Helens is in Washington State.
In 1980, it erupted.

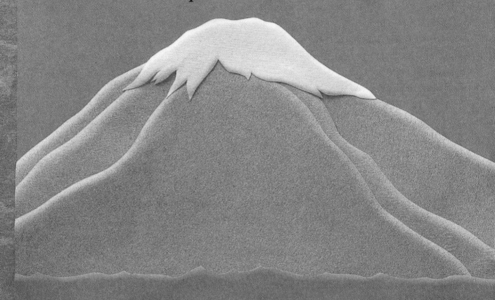

This is Mount St. Helens
before it erupted.

This is Mount St. Helens
after it erupted.

Hawaii has the biggest and busiest
volcanoes in the world.
Mauna Loa is the biggest.
Kilauea is the busiest.
(You say them like this:
maw-na LO-a and ki-lo-AY-a.)
Kilauea has been erupting
on and off for 100 years.
It is called
the "drive-in" volcano.
You can drive or even walk
around its giant crater.
Who knows?
You just might see
a lava fire show there!

Can volcanoes do any good?
Yes.
Over time, ash and lava
turn into rich soil.
The soil is good for farming.

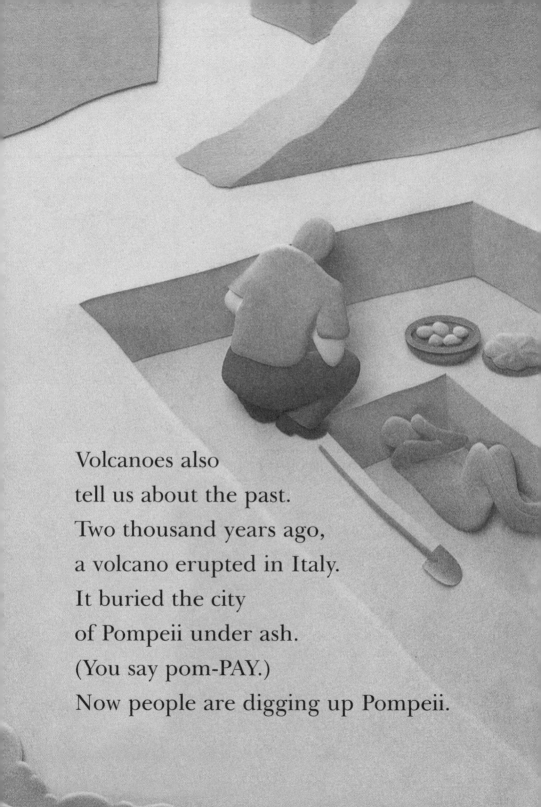

Volcanoes also
tell us about the past.
Two thousand years ago,
a volcano erupted in Italy.
It buried the city
of Pompeii under ash.
(You say pom-PAY.)
Now people are digging up Pompeii.

The ash preserved everything—
even the shapes of the people.

141

Today scientists can usually tell
when a volcano will erupt.
They have special tools.
They watch the movement of the volcano.

They take its temperature.
Sometimes a volcano swells
or the ground gets hot.
Then it is time to watch out!

There are about
500 active volcanoes
in the world.
This map shows
where most of them are found.

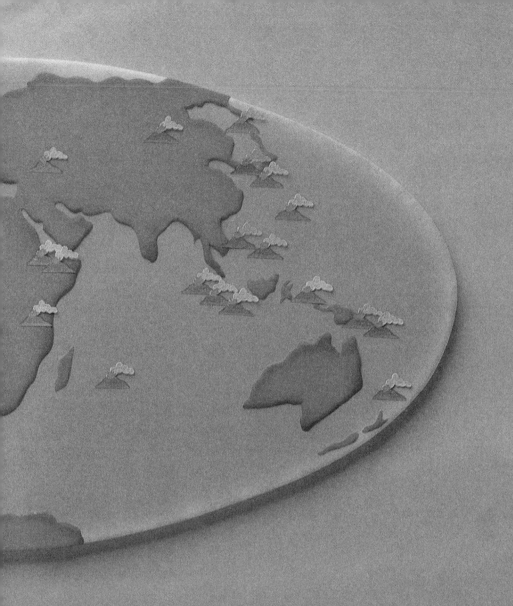

"Active" means the volcano
can erupt at any time.
Other volcanoes are inactive.
They have been dead
for thousands of years.

And then there are volcanoes
that are only sleeping.
Now they are quiet.
But who knows when they will wake up?

STORM CHASERS
Tracking Twisters

By Gail Herman
Illustrated by Larry Schwinger

With photographs

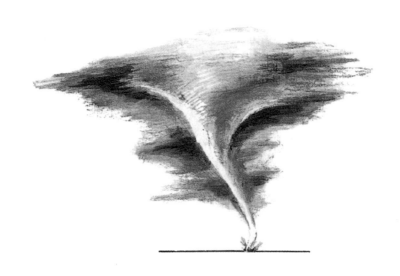

Tornado!

Wee-oh! Wee-oh! Sirens blare. People hurry to a radio or TV and quickly flick it on. Hearts racing, they hear the emergency weather report: "Tornado warning!"

Everywhere, people scurry for shelter. The tornado could hit at any minute. Water is left running. Refrigerators are left open.

Outside all is quiet. Dark, heavy clouds hang in the sky. It is hot. Sticky.

Suddenly, lightning flashes. Thunder booms. A sheet of rain pours down. A minute later, hailstones big as fists clatter to the ground. The wind grows fierce and wild.

The clouds become one giant thunderhead. A point stretches toward the ground.

The point grows longer, and wider. It is a funnel now. The cloud is shaped like an ice-cream cone, or cotton candy on a stick. But it is deadly.

The funnel is twisting. Lower, lower, lower it sinks.

The noise is earthshaking—like thousands of roller coasters bucking and roaring. Inside, in shelters and basements and closets, people cover their ears.

The storm gathers force. Lightning crackles all around. Houses shake. Cars rock.

The funnel spins to the ground. Now it is a huge cloud of twisting, roaring, buzzing dirt and dust—a tornado.

It crashes through houses. It shatters glass. It sweeps away everything it touches.

Trees are plucked right out of the ground. Trucks are tossed high into the air. Roofs are lifted. Buildings crumble. Beams and planks, bricks and furniture fly everywhere.

The tornado races along, smashing everything in its path. Suddenly, it rises. It passes over one block. Then another. House after house is spared. Then it touches down again leaving more homes destroyed. More buildings damaged.

Slowly the tornado shrinks.
It turns long and thin—like a
rope. Seconds later, it disappears.
Everything is still again.
Only minutes have passed. But
the tornado has come and gone.

People come out from hiding. They crawl out from under piles of brick and wood and stone. They look around, dazed.

Houses are broken to bits and pieces. Cars are turned over. Dust and sand litter the ground. Street lights . . . signs . . . everything is ripped out of place, twisted and bent.

People are shocked and still afraid.

And they are lucky. They had time to hide. They had time to run.

But not everyone runs <u>from</u> a tornado. Some people run after them.

Who? Scientists who want to find out more about tornadoes. They want to learn how to tell where and when a tornado will strike. They want to give people more time to find safety.

Who else? Photographers who take pictures of storms. Reporters who are after a good story. People who are interested in weather and want to know more.

Who are these people?

Storm chasers.

Ready for Anything

It's a Sunday in June. A storm chaser named Ross is on his way to the movies. This chaser is also a scientist. He studies weather, and he is called a meteorologist. (You say it like this: mee-tee-or-OL-oh-jist.)

The sky is overcast. It is hot.

Maybe there will be a thunderstorm, Ross thinks. Maybe even a tornado.

He reaches for his car phone. No movie for him. Instead, he calls his partner, Jill.

"Meet me at the weather station!" he tells her excitedly.

At the station, the two scientists pore over computer screens. They check weather information. Temperature. Wind readings.

Warm, damp air is moving up from Mexico. Cold, dry air is moving down from Canada.

Ross and Jill look at one another. If the cold and warm air collide, a tornado can happen.

How? When hot air meets cold air, the cold air slides underneath. The hot air rises. Drops of water are created. And giant thunder clouds form.

Sometimes the hot air gets trapped in the cloud. Sometimes it breaks through with a blast, and the cold air is sent into a whirl. Then a tornado <u>may</u> strike.

Jill and Ross can't be sure. Maybe they'll drive for miles and see nothing. In fact, that's what most chases amount to. But Jill and Ross are willing to take that chance.

The partners rush into a chase car. It is already packed. There are cameras to snap the tornado in action. Maps to help them track it. A laptop computer to get up-to-the-minute information from the weather service. And a tape recorder, so they can remember everything.

The storm chasers are ready for anything. Most of all, they are ready for a tornado.

Tornado Power

Tornado. Twister. Cyclone. Three different names for the same powerful windstorm.

There are other kinds of storms.

Dust devils whirl up from sandy deserts. They are usually small and last only a minute or two.

Waterspouts are tornadoes that form over water. A strong one can pull the water up from a pond—and the fish, too!

Then there are hurricanes—powerful wind and rainstorms. Hurricanes begin over tropical seas. They build slowly over time and last for days and days. Trees are flattened. Buildings are washed away. People abandon their homes as neighborhoods and entire towns are flooded.

Hurricanes have their own chasers.
Hurricane hunters. These hunters risk
their lives every time they venture out
in a storm. Ninety of them have died.

Why?

They fly planes right into the center of
the hurricane. That is how they get
information. The center is calm and still.
But to get there, pilots have to pass
through wild winds of 70 to 100 miles an
hour.

Still, hurricane winds are not nearly as strong as tornado gusts. Tornadoes have the fastest, most dangerous winds on Earth—winds of more than 300 miles an hour!

Tornadoes are also dangerous for a different reason. They strike suddenly— and no one knows where they'll go or what they'll do.

A tornado may speed as fast as 70 miles per hour when it's on the ground. Or it may move slower than a turtle.

A tornado may travel hundreds of miles. Or just a few.

It may last hours. Or just a few seconds.

Sometimes tornadoes attack in groups. One hundred and forty-eight tornadoes struck on the very same day in April 1974. Town after town in midwestern America and Canada was wiped out. More than three hundred people died. They were hit by flying wreckage, buried under houses, flung around by savage winds.

Students at a high school in Ohio were lucky that day. They'd been rehearsing a play on the auditorium stage. One girl glanced out the window and spotted the tornado. The students raced into the hallway, covering their heads. Seconds later, all the school buses blew right onstage.

A man in another town crawled under the couch in his living room. He held onto one couch leg with all his might. The tornado struck his house. Winds gusted all about. When the tornado moved on, the man looked up. He was still clutching that couch leg. But he was outside. There was no house. No furniture. And the rest of the couch had disappeared.

One woman hid in her bathtub. The house flew apart around her. The tub snapped out from the floor. The next thing she knew, the tub turned into a sled. And the woman was sliding into the woods!

Strange things happen during tornadoes. Chickens are plucked clean by the wind. Houses are picked up and turned around—and not even glasses are broken. One man in Wichita, Kansas, was lifted up right into a tornado. He saw tires and a tractor whirling around him. Then he saw a bed—a bed neatly made up with the blanket still tucked in. If only he could reach it, he thought. It looked so comfortable!

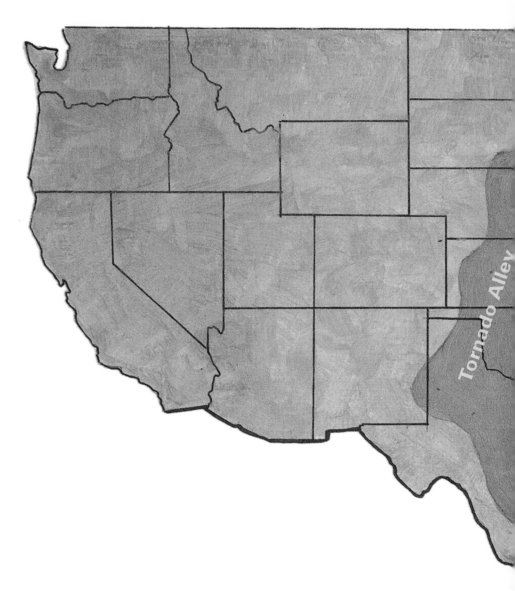

Tornadoes can be big ones or they can be small. About eight hundred tornadoes hit the United States each year. And they've struck all fifty states.

But most tornadoes hit Missouri,

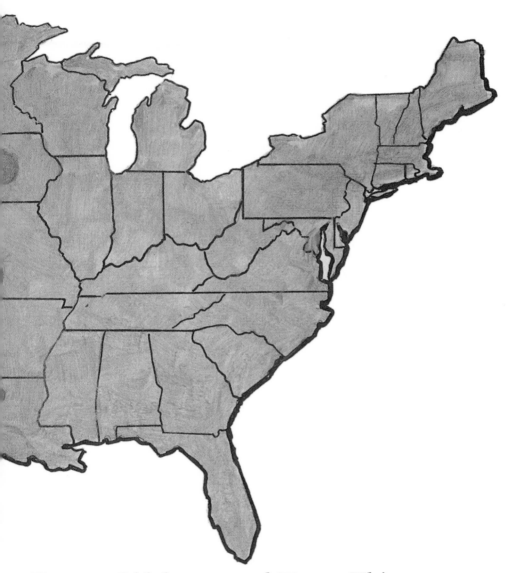

Kansas, Oklahoma, and Texas. This
stretch of land gets so many storms that
it is called Tornado Alley.

And Tornado Alley is where you'll find
storm chasers!

The Chase Is On!

Thunder booms overhead. The rain pours down, and Jill turns on the windshield wipers. The road is wet. Slick. She drives carefully.

She is thinking about another storm chaser. The one who died in a car accident, driving along these same rainsoaked highways.

Giant raindrops splatter on the roof. They run down the windows like waterfalls. Jill squints through the teeming rain. Lightning bolts blind her for seconds at a time. It is tough going.

Clank! Clink! Hailstones hit the car. Whoosh! Wind whistles through the windows. The car shakes, tossed by every gust.

"What should we do?" Ross cries above the noise.

"Find shelter!" Jill shouts.

Four large hailstones

Storm chasing is dangerous, and chasers are always careful. They don't want to be caught in the middle of a storm. The want to see the entire tornado.

"There's an overpass up ahead," Jill says. "I'll get us there."

But the car swerves on the slippery road. The scientist jams the brakes. The car spins. It lurches to a stop. Ross glances out the window.

"Oh no!" he cries. "The tornado!"

A quarter of a mile away . . . about five city blocks . . . the big swirling cloud of dust and dirt looms up.

The scientists are so close they can't see the top. They are so close they can't see the bottom. They just see something dark and big. Something turning, turning, turning.

Jill hits the gas. Ross looks for a ditch—someplace to take cover.

The black smoky column snakes farther away. It spins into the distance, out of sight.

The wind dies down. The shaking stops.

The scientists pull over.

"Whew!" says Ross. "That was close! We didn't even see it!"

The tornado loomed larger than a towering mountain! How could they have missed it? Easy. It was wrapped in rain.

The rain covered the twister like a blanket. So the chasers didn't see it—until they were almost in it.

Both scientists take deep breaths. They check their laptop for information. The storm is moving north. And so are they.

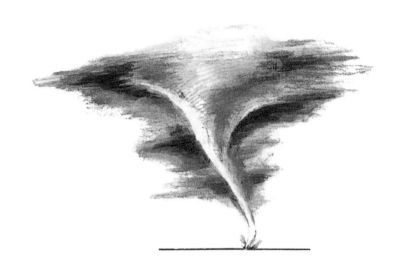

The Chasers

People have always chased storms. There were just a few chasers at first. They were drawn to storms—to their strange beauty and their force. They loved seeing nature at its most powerful.

They would roam the plains of the Midwest. They would go out in late spring, searching and searching.

These people weren't trained. They weren't even scientists. But they did take pictures. They took notes about clouds and temperatures. And when they saw a tornado form, they would call the sheriff or the police. They would start the warning.

Some scientists took notice. Maybe these storm chasers were onto something, they thought. So they went into the field too.

Scientists had lots of ideas. Could they fly a rocket into a tornado? Maybe a plane without any crew? No, they decided. Those ideas wouldn't work.

But they could try something else. They could try and place special instruments in the path of a tornado. These instruments could help them learn about tornadoes close up.

First scientists tried TOTO. TOTO was an invention named after the dog in "The Wizard of Oz." But this TOTO was a weather station. It looked like a giant garbage can. And it weighed 400 pounds.

Scientists had to carry TOTO to the storm in a pickup truck. Then five people had to haul it out. TOTO was that heavy. In fact, TOTO was <u>too</u> heavy. It took too much time to set up. And the tornado could close in at any second. So scientists came up with another invention—Turtles.

Turtles are small flat packages loaded with instruments. They are much easier to set up than TOTO.

Turtles are what scientists used in their latest project: VORTEX. In 1994 and 1995, science teams combed Oklahoma, Texas, and Kansas looking for tornadoes. They piled into vans and cars with rooftop weather stations.

Pilots jumped into planes. They followed the storm. Their job? To help out the ground crews. How big was the tornado? How fast was it moving? From way up high, they could answer these questions.

Scientists let loose huge balloons—balloons with measuring instruments dangling from them. Whoosh! Up they would fly. They would be tossed by heavy winds and carried higher and higher still. Then, pop! The balloons would burst. Parachutes would open, and carry the instruments to Earth.

These instruments told scientists about the air and temperature way up high. And the balloons also told scientists about wind speed and direction.

Scientists learned a lot from each tornado they tracked. But more work needs to be done. Tornadoes are still a mystery. A mystery that needs to be solved.

When a Tornado Hits

You're listening to the radio. Suddenly you hear the news. There's a severe storm heading your way. It's a tornado watch!

You run to the windows. The skies are dark. It starts to rain. Thunder booms in the distance. The clouds hang low. A funnel seems to form.

What do you do?

You keep listening . . . to the radio or TV, whether you're at home or at school. It is important to know if the tornado watch changes into a tornado warning.

That means a tornado has actually been spotted. Or radar has picked it up for certain.

Don't use the telephone. There is lots and lots of lightning and electricity during these storms. You could get a shock from the wires.

If you are home, go to the basement. Get under the stairs or a piece of heavy furniture.

What if you don't have a basement? Get in a closet in the middle of your home. Kneel on the floor facing a wall. Put your hands over your head.

At school, stay away from gyms and auditoriums. Big rooms like these can collapse in an instant.

If you are outside, find a hiding place that is lower than the ground. A ditch or a hole would be good. Then lie down and cover your head.

If you are in a car, get out. It is hard to drive faster than a tornado. Again, take cover in a ditch.

And if you ever think of chasing a tornado—or any kind of storm—think again. Only experts should go storm chasing.

Remember, a tornado may be exciting. But its power can destroy homes and lives.

TERROR BELOW!
True Shark Stories

By Dana del Prado
Illustrated by Stephen Marchesi

Are you afraid of sharks? Lots of people are. But you don't have to worry about them every time you go swimming. Shark attacks happen much less often in real life than they do in books or movies. In fact, there are fewer than 100 shark attacks a year in the whole world. Bee stings kill more people than sharks do.

Actually, sharks have more to fear from humans than the other way around. People kill hundreds of millions of sharks every year. Some are eaten as food. Some are caught by accident in giant fishing nets. And some are hunted just for fun.

Many people think the world would be better off without sharks. But sharks do a lot of good. They help keep the ocean clean by eating up dead, sick, and weak animals—from tiny fish to huge whales. Some scientists believe that studying sharks will help them develop life-saving medicines.

Of course, sharks <u>are</u> dangerous. Hopefully, the three stories in this book are the closest you'll ever come to one!

Big and Little

The largest fish in the world is a shark—the whale shark. It grows to 35 or 40 feet, longer than a bus. Its mouth alone is six feet wide! But it is harmless. The whale shark has even let divers ride on its back.

The tiniest shark is only six inches long. It has a very long name, tsurana-gakobitosame. (It's fun to try to say it: Sur-AH-na-gak-oh-BIT-oh-SAH-mee.) This is Japanese for "little shark with a long face."

The Big Three

There are about 350 different kinds
of sharks. New kinds are always being
discovered. Luckily, only a few types
attack people. These are the most
dangerous:

great white
shark

bull shark

tiger shark

Are there other dangerous sharks? Yes.
But these are less likely to bother humans:

dusky

lemon

gray reef

hammerhead

mako

Hawaii, 1992

It was 7:30 in the morning. Rick had the beach all to himself. Not a soul was out. Soon he had to be at his job as a building worker. But he figured he had time to catch a few waves. That was the great thing about living in Hawaii. The surf was always nearby.

Huge breakers were crashing into shore. Rick grabbed his surfboard and dove in. Seconds later, he was riding a big wave. He caught another, and another.

There was just time for one more ride before work. Rick floated on his board waiting for the next really big one. As he drifted, he looked down into the clear blue water. A dark shape glided near him. It was a giant green sea turtle. Rick was a nature-lover. He knew he was very lucky to have seen such a rare sea creature.

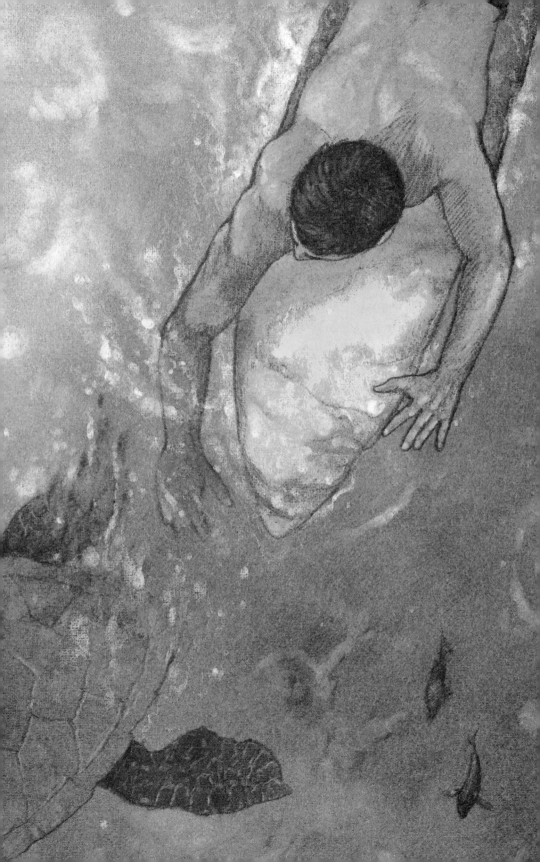

Rick was still smiling when a larger
shadow drifted by. He couldn't quite make
it out. It wasn't a sea turtle. But what was
it? Then the water swirled. Up rose an
enormous tiger shark!

The shark opened its huge jaws. Rick
could see row after row of jagged white
teeth. Then those teeth came down hard.
The shark bit into Rick's surfboard! The
board swung up and down, back and
forth as the shark shook it. Rick just held
on tight with his arms and legs.

Suddenly Rick heard a loud SNAP. The tiger shark had bitten right through the board!

Rick knew he had to act . . . fast! He started paddling for shore. It felt like the longest swim of his life.

Finally he was there. A crowd was waiting. A busload of tourists had stopped to see what was going on in the water.

Rick was still scared. He hadn't been hurt at all. But one look at his chomped board was enough to start him shaking.

Why had the shark gone after the board and not Rick? Rick had no idea. But he was sure of one thing. He was very lucky.

Yum

What do sharks eat? Almost anything!
All these things have been found inside
sharks' stomachs:

tin cans
a crocodile head
a wallet
a drum
cigarette packs
nuts and bolts
a suit of armor
a fur coat

Australia, 1937

Iona had an unusual job. He was a pearl diver. Every day he swam the waters off the Great Barrier Reef in Australia, looking for oysters. He brought up hundreds in hopes of finding one that would hold a pearl.

One morning he dropped off the dive boat as usual. The water was warm and clear. It was easy to see oysters on rocks and in branches of white coral. There was a big one! Iona pried it off, then swam back up and left his catch in a bucket. He didn't open the oyster right then. He would do that later.

Down Iona went again. He swam
slowly, searching hard for more oysters.
Then, out of nowhere, a shadow appeared
on the ocean floor. It loomed up behind
him. Iona turned.

He was face-to-face with a giant tiger
shark.

In a flash, the shark opened his huge
jaws and clamped them down around
Iona's neck. His head was inside the
shark's great dark mouth!

Iona was still alive. But he felt the shark's teeth closing down on him. He had just seconds to fight back. And he knew what to do. He felt around the shark's head. With all his strength, he stuck his thumbs deep into the shark's eyes! He pushed deeper and deeper. The shark thrashed in the water. Then it let go!

Iona was free. He sprang up to the surface. The other divers pulled him onto the dive boat. He was badly hurt. His neck was ringed with deep cuts.

There was no time to lose. The crew rushed Iona to the nearest hospital. It took 100 stitches to fix his wound.

The shark left scars around Iona's throat—like a necklace. But Iona was okay. He could go back to pearl diving. He even had something to remember that horrible day. It wasn't a pearl. It was a shark's tooth. Doctors had found it buried deep in Iona's neck.

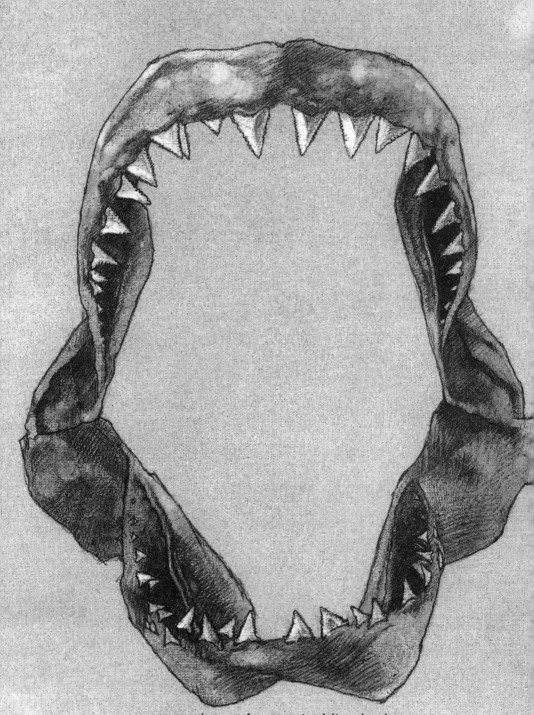

jaws of a great white shark

Teeth

A shark may lose thousands of teeth in its lifetime—some lose about a tooth a week. But sharks always have plenty of teeth. New ones keep taking the place of the teeth that fall out.

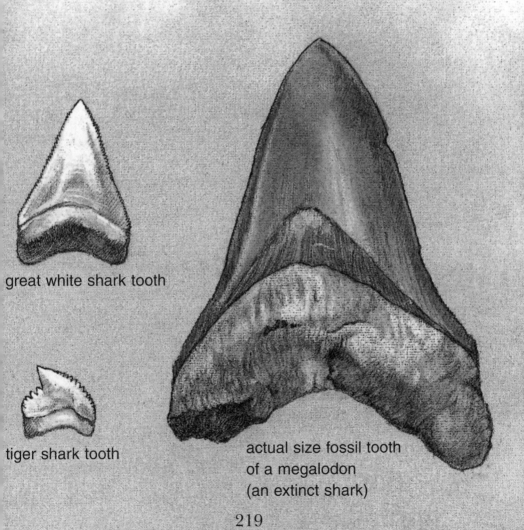

great white shark tooth

tiger shark tooth

actual size fossil tooth of a megalodon (an extinct shark)

Shark Chaser

Wouldn't it be great to have a pill that you could drop into the water—and make sharks go away from you? The U.S. Navy actually came up with one in the 1940s. It was called Shark Chaser. There was a problem, though. Shark Chaser did not work on all kinds of sharks. And it was useless against a feeding frenzy—when a group of hungry, excited sharks attack together.

South Australia, 1963

More than anything, Rodney wanted to win the spearfishing championship. He had won the year before. He knew he could do it again.

But so far he had had hardly any luck. He hadn't caught much at all. To take first place he'd have to bring down a truly huge fish.

Suddenly, Rodney saw a dusky morwong—it was big. This could win him the contest! The fish was just ahead of him. Rodney lifted his spear and took a shot.

He missed. The morwong swam off with a flip of its tail.

There were only minutes left in the contest. Rodney knew it was now or never. He caught sight of a school of barracuda. This was his chance. He moved after them. Behind him the water was strangely still. At first he kept his eyes on the barracuda. But the quiet started to bother him. He looked over his shoulder.

There was a great white shark! Before
Rodney could get away, the shark's huge
mouth closed over his chest and back.

Terrified, Rodney used his free hand to beat at the shark's head. But the thick-skinned shark barely noticed. It shook Rodney back and forth in the water. Rodney tried to claw at the shark's black unblinking eye. But his hand slipped and his arm went straight into the shark's mouth. Still full of fight, Rodney tore his arm back out.

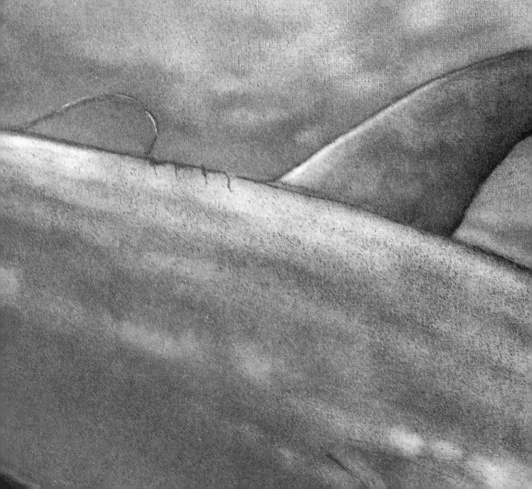

For the first time that day, Rodney had some luck. The great white let go. But it hadn't given up. The killer came after Rodney again. This time it gripped on a float tied to Rodney's dive belt. The float was filled with dead fish Rodney used to attract his spearfishing targets.

Down, down the shark dragged him in the water. Rodney grabbed for the catch to undo his belt. Then the shark's razorlike teeth sawed through the line. Free once more, Rodney used the last of his strength to swim to the surface.

Luckily, a dive boat was just yards away. The crew pulled Rodney out of the water and onto the deck. He was bleeding badly.

The boat raced to shore. Soon Rodney was rushed to the nearest hospital. There a doctor worked on him for four hours. It took 462 stitches to save Rodney's life.

After a day like that, you would think Rodney would hate sharks. Not at all. Today he fights to protect them. And he runs a dive shop that takes people out to get a close look at sharks in the wild. Just not <u>too</u> close.

Doctor Shark

Sharks are healthy animals. Their wounds heal fast. They almost never get cancer. So scientists study sharks to learn new ways to help cure people.

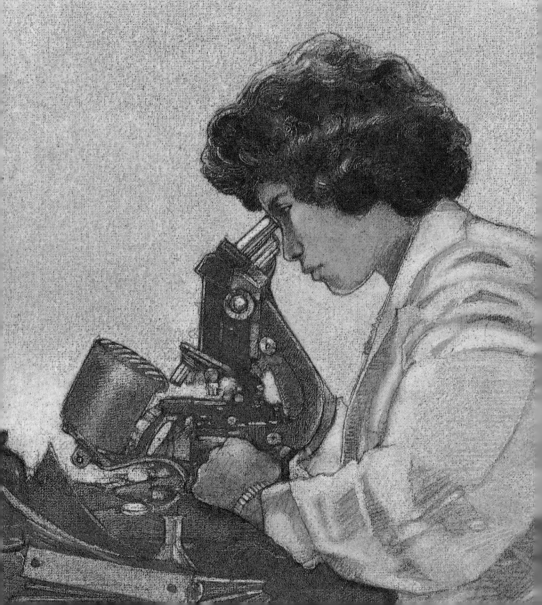

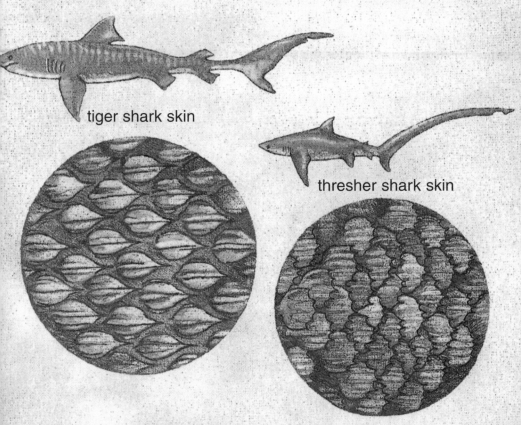

tiger shark skin

thresher shark skin

Shark Skin: Never Pet a Shark!

Did you know you can cut yourself
on a shark's skin? That has actually
happened to some swimmers. How?
A shark's skin is covered with sharp
toothlike prickles. If you pet a shark (a
bad idea!) from its head toward its tail, it
would feel smooth. Pet it from its tail
toward its head and—ouch!

Swimming with Sharks

If you play it safe, you can reduce the chance of a close encounter of the worst kind. Here are five rules to remember when swimming in places where sharks have been spotted:

1) Never swim alone.
2) Never swim with an open wound. Blood attracts sharks.
3) Never swim at night or at sunset.
4) Leave the water right away if a shark is spotted. Swim as smoothly as possible.
5) Never grab or injure any shark.